FRANCIS STERLING HAYDEN DUSTIN HOFFMAN ORSON

FORD ALFRED HITCHCOCK WELLES

BARBARA STANWYCK HUMPHREY JOEL

COPPOLA FRANÇOIS JAMES BOGART McCREA

TRUFFAUT WOODY MARILYN

ROBERT DeNIRO ALLEN STEWART MONROE

FAYE

MICHAEL

CURTIZ WES ANDERSON DUNAWAY CARY GRANT MONROE

NAME *That* MOVIE

100 Illustrated Movie Puzzles

by PAUL ROGERS

CHRONICLE BOOKS
SAN FRANCISCO

Library of Congress Cataloging-in-Publication Data available
ISBN 978-1-4521-0497-3

Manufactured in China

Designed by Jill von Hartmann

10 9 8 7

Chronicle Books LLC
680 Second Street
San Francisco CA 94107
www.chroniclebooks.com

Chronicle Books publishes distinctive books and gifts. From award-winning children's titles, best-selling cookbooks, and eclectic pop culture to acclaimed works of art and stationery, and journals, we craft publishing that's instantly recognizable for its spirit and creativity. Enjoy our publishing and become part of our community at www.chroniclebooks.com.

FOR THOSE WONDERFUL PEOPLE
OUT THERE IN THE DARK.

INTRODUCTION

While watching *Chinatown* for about the fiftieth time—during the scene when Gittes places two watches under the tire of Hollis Mulwray's car—it occurred to me that if I made a drawing of the watches and the tire, people who love the movie would recognize that small moment in the film. This led to the idea that a series of drawings made from classic films might make an interesting visual quiz. Soon, I began re-watching some of my favorite movies with a sketchbook and pausing the film to make drawings.

For the most part, I tried to avoid the most obvious scenes and stars who might give away the title too easily and instead, concentrated on details that appealed to me. As a graphic designer who particularly loves architecture and typography, I found myself paying close attention to buildings and signs. Also, lettering—large or small—always jumped out at me. I hadn't noticed until I started working on this book how frequently handwritten notes or pieces of printed paper appear as important elements of the plot.

I found that six drawings in sequence could give a nice sense of the film. The goal was to give hints that spark the memory of a film rather than tell the whole story. Of course, some of the movies had dozens of great shots for drawings and it was a challenge to pick just six, while others required much deeper scrutiny.

The movies in this book are all films that I love. Some of them I'm certain everyone has seen, while others may have slipped from public awareness; but they're all great. There's a lot of Hitchcock (hint), and Billy Wilder, some vintage film noir and recent box office hits, a few foreign films, and somehow, a lot of films from the seventies. Some of my favorite movies didn't make the cut because they might be a little too obscure to work well in this puzzle context (hard to guess a film you haven't seen or heard of), but I will say that if you haven't seen *Pickup on South Street* (1953) and *Elevator to the Gallows* (1958) you should!

There are one hundred movies in this book. The answers are given in two places in the back. There's a list of titles in the order that they appear in the book and there's also an alphabetical index. The alphabetical index is there for readers who don't want to inadvertently see the next title on the list when checking the answers. I hope you enjoy the book and find yourself paying a bit more attention to those small moments that make up great films.

I'd like to add a word of appreciation to my wife Jill, who tolerated a lot of Sunday afternoons while I sat on the sofa in front of the television with a sketchbook and the remote control. Now that the book's finished, we can go out on Sundays and maybe see a movie.

—*Paul Rogers*

Balls models

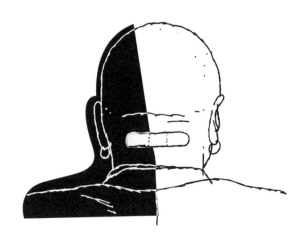

DRIVE IN
RIVER GLEN MOTEL

MOTEL
VACANCY

20933
MONEY
TO
LOAN

Buy
Sell
Trade

INSTANT CASH
JEWELRY · GOLD · DIAMONDS
TV · VCR · TOOLS · WATCHES
STEREO · CAMERA

LOAN

Hawthorne GRILL

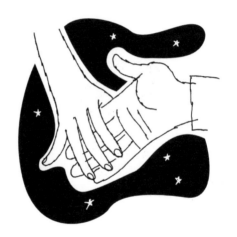

BATON ROUGE, LOUISIANA

WHERE IS HE?

NO TRACE SINCE HE FLED DYING BROTHER

U.S. Delegates Attend Meet

LOVE

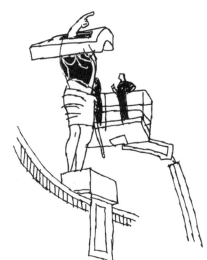

DEATH LIST FIVE

① OREN ISHII
   COTTONMOUTH

② VERNITA GREEN
   COPPERHEAD

③ BUDD
   SIDE WINDER

④ ELLE DRIVER
   CALIFORNIA MOUNTAIN SNAKE

⑤ B

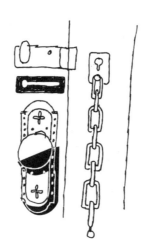

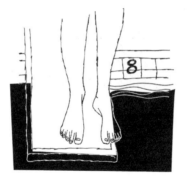

CLOSED
GONE TO
HANGING
R. Ryan

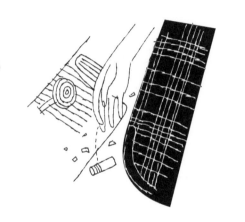

**GRAND JURY INDICTS
CHAMBERS AS SLAYER**

Killed Wife In Bogus
Auto Accident, Charge
To Face Murder Trial

Sensational Cora Smith Case
Has Aftermath in Action
Against Husband

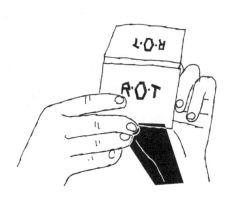

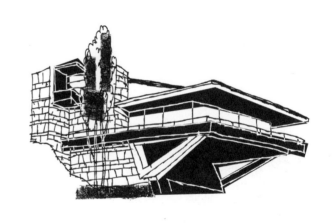

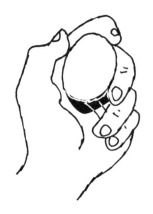

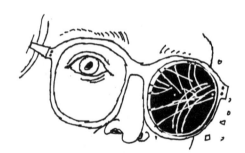

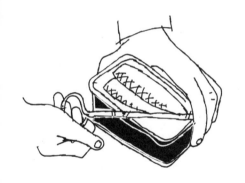  

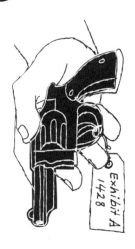

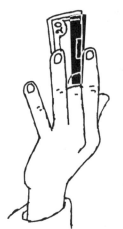

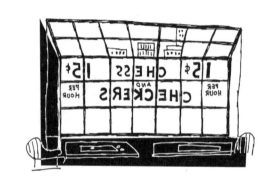

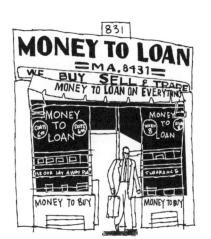

24

831

MONEY TO LOAN

══ MA. 8431 ══

WE BUY SELL & TRADE

MONEY TO LOAN ON EVERYTHING

MONEY TO LOAN

COATS 6⁹⁵ SUITS 6⁹⁵

USE OUR LAY AWAY PLAN

MONEY TO LOAN

WASH 8 GUN

CLEARANCE

MONEY TO BUY

MONEY TO BUY

FLAMINGO

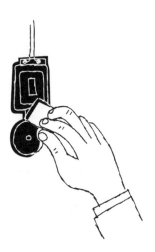  

DEBONAIR
SOCIAL CLUB

MEMBERS ONLY

An Evening
WITH
JAKE LA MOTTA
featuring the works
of
• PADDY CHAYEFSKY
• ROD SERLING
• SHAKESPEARE
• BUDD SCHULBERG
• TENNESSEE WILLIAMS

Tonight

28

We better get going if we going to stay ahead of the weather

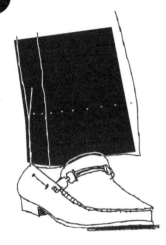

DEFENSE D'AFFICHER

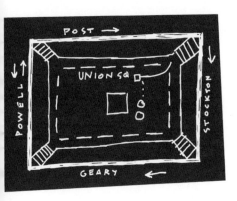

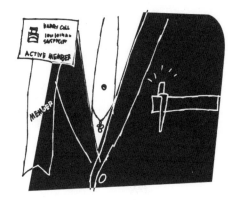

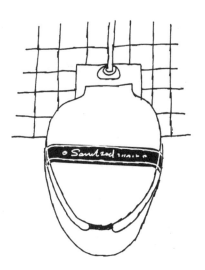

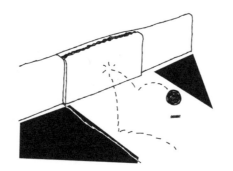

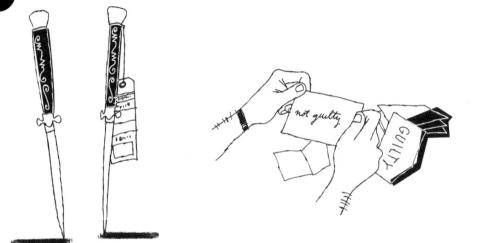

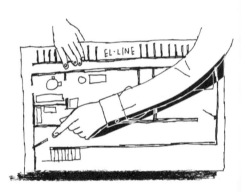

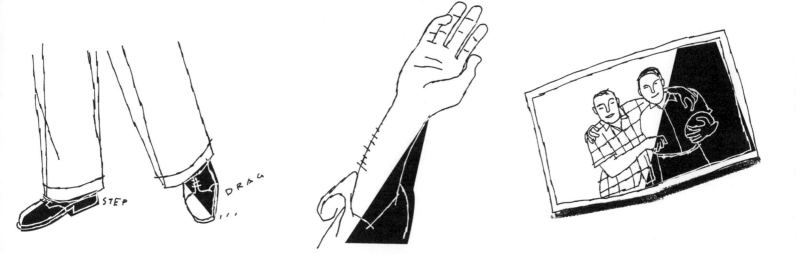

J.J. Hunsecker

Get
Harry
Kells
Tonight

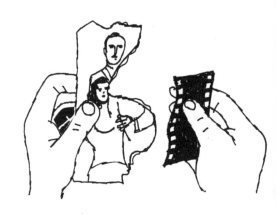

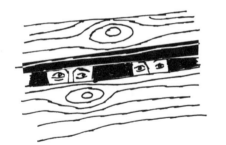

Elaine's

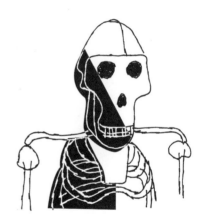

पाश्चात्य शौली
WESTERN STYLE

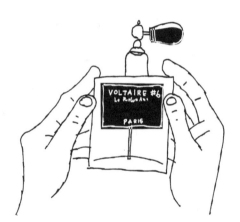

VOLTAIRE #6
Le Roymeaux

PARIS

TRANSMISSIONS

ENGINE

Shock

SPRING

Luftwaffe Automotive
Specialists in Fine German Motor Cars

30-56

CNJ 314

41

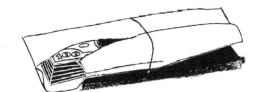

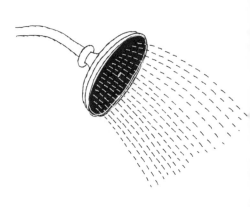

DIME AND SPY
INCORPORATED

SIDNEY KIDD

EDITOR AND PUBLISHER

CLICK

PUBLIC LIBRARY
OPEN DAILY
9 AM to 5 PM
WED. EVENINGS
7 PM to 8 PM

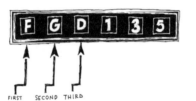

FIRST   SECOND THIRD

 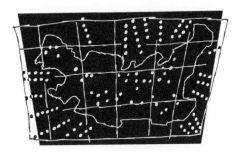 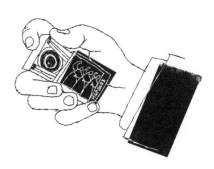

Ellis Boyd Redding/30265
Determination

REJECTED

His Judgement Cometh
and that Right Soon....

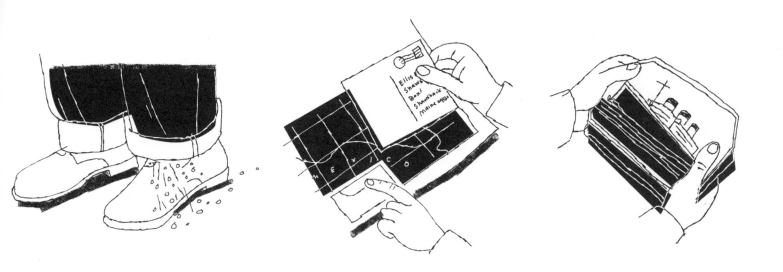

NOT TOO LOUD!
THE NEIGHBORS
ARE COMPLAINING

THE MUSIC MAN

"ONE OF THE BEST MUSICAL COMEDIES OF OUR TIMES"

C.C. BAXTER
2nd ADMINISTRATIVE
ASSISTANT

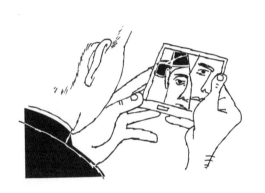

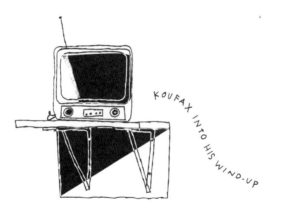

KOUFAX INTO HIS WIND-UP

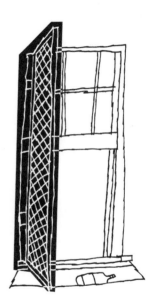

BOOKENDS SIMON & GARFUNKEL

Continental HYATT HOUSE

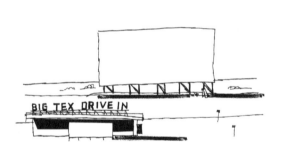

Kansas City Tribune

STRANGE DEATH OF HOLLYWOOD DIRECTOR

PROMINENT CITIZENS ALONG WITH CIVIC BODIES COMBINE TO MAKE CITY PARK SUCCESS

Accord Reached Farm Payments

JOHN L. SULLIVAN FOUND DEAD IN FREIGHT YARDS

O BROTHER WHERE ART THOU?

BY Sinclair Beckstein

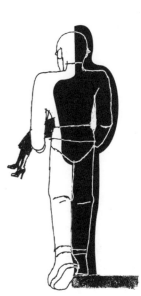

San Francisco Post-Dispatch

THURSBY, ARCHER MURDERS LINKED

CONSERVATIVES HALT CONFIRMATION MOVE | FEDERAL R REPORTS CHANGES) | Private Detective Was Shadowing Thursby.

PASSPORT

Joel Cairo

SHIPPING NEWS

Arriving Today

5:35 P.M – La Paloma from Hong Kong

6:20 P.M.– Shasta King from Seattle

STAGE · BROADWAY · SCREEN

VARIETY

25 CENTS

STUDIOS CONVERT TO TALKIES

| BEST RESTAURANT ON B'WAY STARTS ON SHOESTRING | MAD SCRAMBLE ON FOR SOUND | SOCK BIZ FOR LEGIT NOW—BUT MOVIES STILL STIFF |

VOWEL E

HOTEL ASTOR · ASTOR HOTEL · SARDI'S · STRAND · Casino · PALACE · Gaiety · LOEW'S · LOEW'S STATE · CRITERION

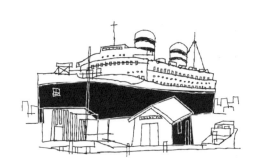

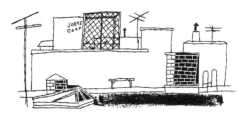

  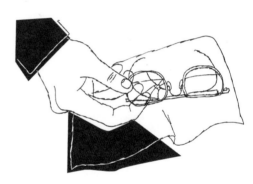

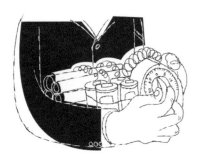

WELCOME STRANGER! TO PICTURESQUE LOS ROBLES
THE PARIS OF THE BORDER

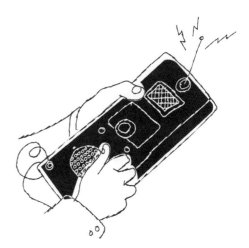

60

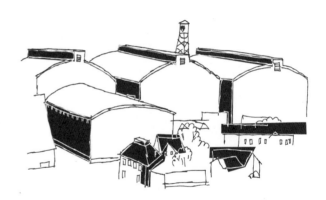

 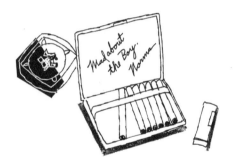 

Mad about the Boy. Norma

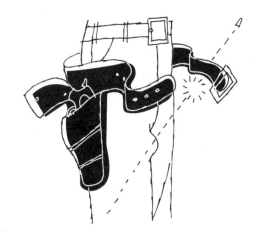

STEAMSHIP
Passage to
South America

NEW YORK TRAVEL
COMPANY

63

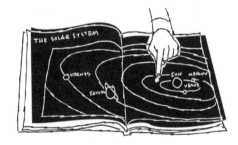

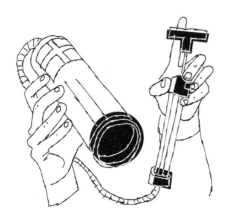

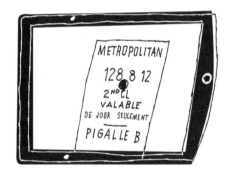

69

METROPOLITAN
128 8 12
2ND CL
VALABLE
DE JOUR SEULEMENT
PIGALLE B

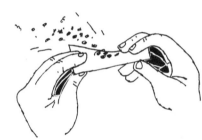

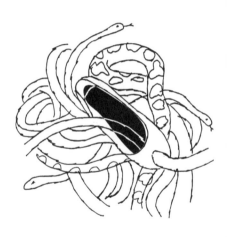

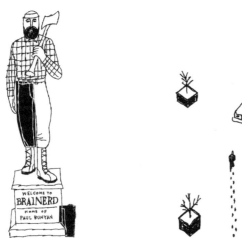

WELCOME TO
BRAINERD
HOME OF
PAUL BUNYAN

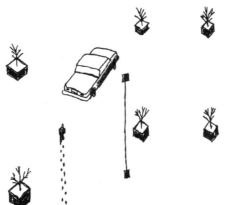

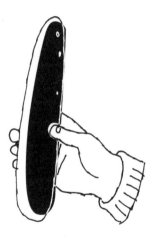

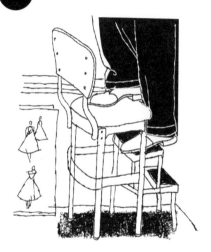

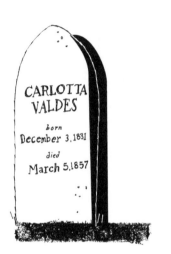

72

CARLOTTA
VALDES

born
December 3, 1831

died
March 5, 1857

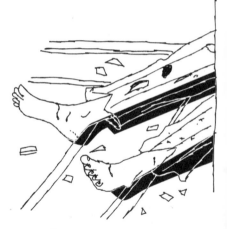

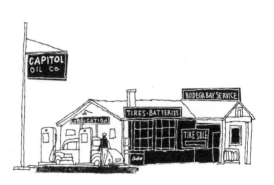

285

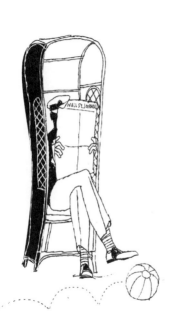

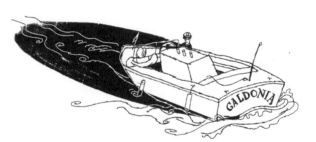

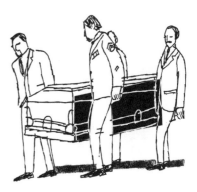

THE SORROW
AND
THE PITY

© CINEMA 5 LTD, 1972

© MARCEL OPHULS, ANDRE HARRIS, 1969

100 FPI
NEW YORK

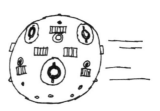

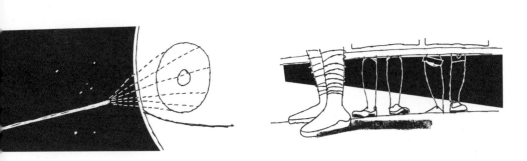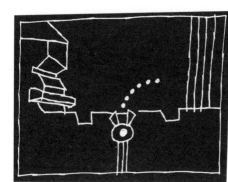

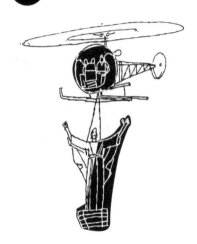

acqua
S.PELLEGRINO

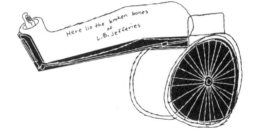

Here lie the broken bones
of
L.B. Jefferies

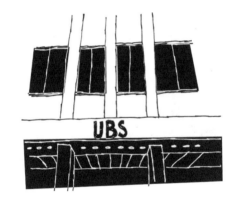

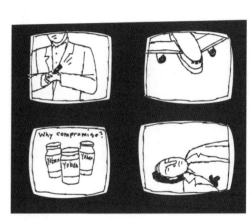

 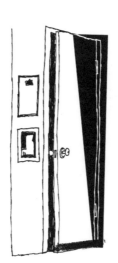 

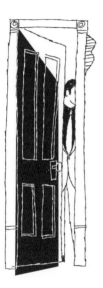

92

The BOOK of the FILM

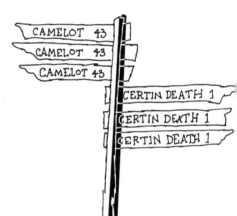

CAMELOT 43
CAMELOT 43
CAMELOT 43

CERTIN DEATH 1
CERTIN DEATH 1
CERTIN DEATH 1

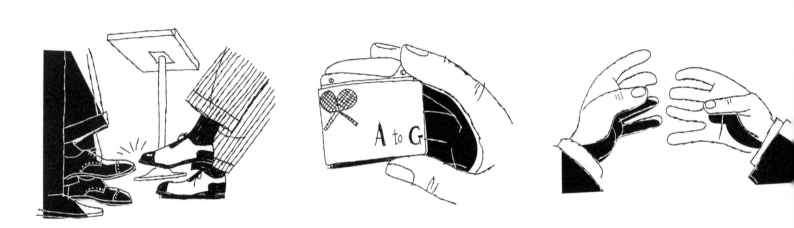

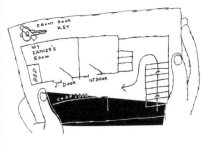 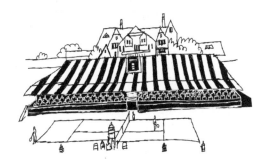 

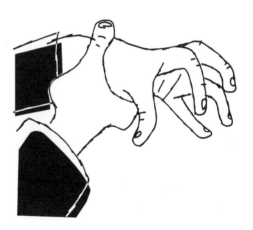

93

95

To John
from Margaret
The Lord bless thee
and keep thee

Easter 1928

THE CHURCH HYMNAL
REVISED EDITION

PALLADIUM
CRAZY MONTH

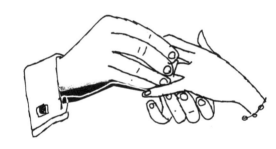

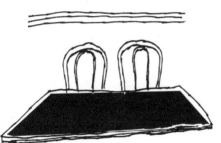

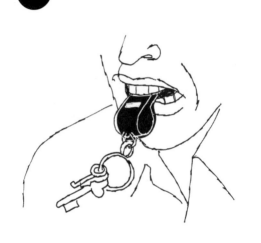

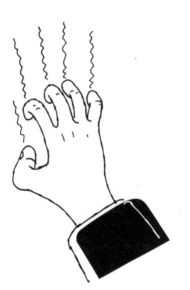

  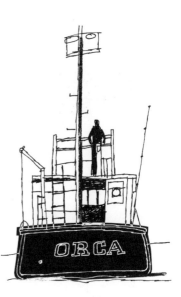

  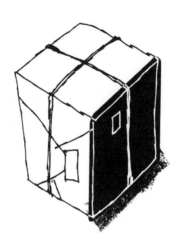

99

3 Years Dead

H. DELBRUCK

Bucharest Academy of Science
TONIGHT ONLY
DR. F. FRANKENSTEIN
PRESENTS
THE CREATURE
IN
"A Startling New Experiment in R..."
PRESENTED IN COOPERA...
TNS
(Transylvania Ne...

SOLD OUT

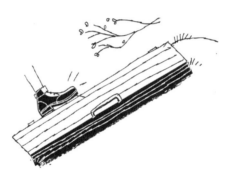

ANSWERS

1 Casablanca (1942)

 2 Zoolander (2001)

 3 Pulp Fiction (1994)

 4 Titanic (1997)

 5 Bonnie and Clyde (1967)

 6 The Godfather (1972)

 7 The Hangover (2009)

 8 The Sting (1973)

 9 Kill Bill Vol. 1 (2003)

 10 The Big Lebowski (1998)

 11 Bullitt (1968)

 12 Goodfellas (1990)

13 Taxi Driver (1976)

 14 The Last Picture Show (1971)

 15 True Grit (1969)

 16 Clerks (1994)

 17 The Postman Always Rings Twice (1946)

 18 North by Northwest (1959)

 19 The Graduate (1967)

 20 Cool Hand Luke (1967)

 21 The Tin Drum (1979)

 22 Mildred Pierce (1945)

 23 The Grifters (1990)

 24 The Killing (1956)

25 Double Indemnity (1944)

 26 The Third Man (1949)

 27 Raging Bull (1980)

 28 Groundhog Day (1993)

 29 Anchorman: The Legend of Ron Burgundy (2004)

 30 Citizen Kane (1941)

 31 Day for Night (1973)

 32 The Conversation (1974)

 33 Amélie (2001)

 34 12 Angry Men (1957)

 35 The Big Sleep (1946)

 36 Sweet Smell of Success (1957)

37 Cinema Paradiso (1988)

 38 Inglourious Basterds (2009)

 39 Manhattan (1979)

 40 The Darjeeling Limited (2007)

 41 Reservoir Dogs (1992)

 42 Psycho (1960)

 43 The Philadelphia Story (1940)

 44 Dr. Strangelove (1964)

 45 The Shawshank Redemption (1994)

 46 The Apartment (1960)

 47 One Flew Over the Cuckoo's Nest (1975)

 48 Almost Famous (2000)

49 The Royal Tenenbaums (2001)

 50 Midnight Cowboy (1969)

 51 Sullivan's Travels (1941)

 52 The Day the Earth Stood Still (1951)

 53 The Maltese Falcon (1941)

 54 Singin' in the Rain (1952)

 55 Do the Right Thing (1989)

 56 On the Waterfront (1954)

 57 Chinatown (1974)

 58 Touch of Evil (1958)

 59 Breathless (1960)

 60 The Red Shoes (1948)

61 Blazing Saddles (1974)

 **62** Sunset Blvd. (1950)

 63 Butch Cassidy and the Sundance Kid (1969)

 64 E.T.: The Extra-Terrestrial (1982)

 65 Modern Times (1936)

 66 Austin Powers: International Man of Mystery (1997)

 67 Boogie Nights (1997)

 68 Pee-Wee's Big Adventure (1985)

 69 The Wages of Fear (1953)

 70 Raiders of the Lost Ark (1981)

 71 Fargo (1996)

 72 Animal House (1978)

73 Vertigo (1958)

 74 Fast Times at Ridgemont High (1982)

 75 The Birds (1963)

 76 Dog Day Afternoon (1975)

 77 Some Like It Hot (1959)

 78 Saturday Night Fever (1977)

 79 Giant (1956)

 80 The Deer Hunter (1978)

 81 Annie Hall (1977)

 82 Ferris Bueller's Day Off (1986)

 83 Star Wars: Episode IV – A New Hope (1977)

 84 La Dolce Vita (1960)

85 Rear Window (1954)

 86 Network (1976)

 **87** Three Days of the Condor (1975)

 88 O Brother, Where Art Thou? (2000)

 89 Broadway Danny Rose (1984)

 90 Diner (1982)

 91 Guys and Dolls (1955)

 92 Monty Python and the Holy Grail (1974)

 93 Strangers on a Train (1951)

 94 To Kill a Mockingbird (1962)

 95 The 39 Steps (1935)

96 The Umbrellas of Cherbourg (1964)

97 Jaws (1975)

 98 Barton Fink (1991)

 99 Young Frankenstein (1974)

 100 The Wizard of Oz (1939)

MOVIE INDEX

Diner (1982) — **90**

Do the Right Thing (1989) — **55**

Dog Day Afternoon (1975) — **76**

Double Indemnity (1944) — **25**

Dr. Strangelove (1964) — **44**

E

E.T.: The Extra-Terrestrial (1982) — **64**

F

Fargo (1996) — **71**

Fast Times at Ridgemont High (1982) — **74**

Ferris Bueller's Day Off (1986) — **82**

G

Giant (1956) — **79**

The Godfather (1972) — **6**

Goodfellas (1990) — **12**

The Graduate (1967) — **19**

The Grifters (1990) — **23**

Groundhog Day (1993) — **28**

Guys and Dolls (1955) — **91**

H

The Hangover (2009) — **7**

I

Inglourious Basterds (2009) — **38**

J

Jaws (1975) — **97**

K

Kill Bill Vol. 1 (2003) — **9**

The Killing (1956) — **24**

L

La Dolce Vita (1960) — **84**

The Last Picture Show (1971) — **14**

M

The Maltese Falcon (1941) — **53**

Manhattan (1979) — **39**

Midnight Cowboy (1969) — **50**

T

12 Angry Men (1957) — **34**

The 39 Steps (1935) — **95**

Taxi Driver (1976) — **13**

The Third Man (1949) — **26**

Three Days of the Condor
  (1975) — **87**

The Tin Drum (1979) — **21**

Titanic (1997) — **4**

To Kill a Mockingbird (1962) — **94**

Touch of Evil (1958) — **58**

True Grit (1969) — **15**

U

The Umbrellas of Cherbourg
  (1964) — **96**

V

Vertigo (1958) — **73**

W

The Wages of Fear (1953) — **69**

Wizard of Oz (1939) — **100**

Y

Young Frankenstein (1974) — **99**

Z

Zoolander (2001) — **2**

PAUL ROGERS IS AN ILLUSTRATOR AND GRAPHIC DESIGNER WHOSE WORK HAS BEEN FEATURED IN NUMEROUS PUBLICATIONS AND A VARIETY OF POPULAR CHILDREN'S BOOKS, AS WELL AS ON POSTAGE STAMPS AND ICONIC POSTERS FOR THE U.S. OPEN AND THE LOS ANGELES DODGERS. HE LIVES IN PASADENA, CALIFORNIA.

PAUL NEWMAN QUENTIN TARANTINO WARREN JEFF

JOSEPH COTTEN BILLY WILDER BEATTY JEFF

STANLEY JACK NICHOLSON SHIRLEY MARTIN BRIDGES

KUBRICK JANET LEIGH JEAN-LUC GODARD MacLAINE SCORSESE JACK

PRESTON STURGES AL PACINO LEMMON

WILLIAM MEL BROOKS JOHN CAZALE

HOLDEN STEVEN GRACE ROMAN

SPIELBERG JOHN HOUSTON KELLY POLANSKI